THE
LIFE & DEATH
OF THE
CHESAPEAKE
BAY

J.R. SCHUBEL

A Maryland Sea Grant Publication
University of Maryland
College Park

Fourth printing, 1996.
All photographs by J.R. Schubel.
Book design by Sandy Harpe.

Publication Number
UM-SG-MP-86-01

The publication of this series is made possible in part by a grant from the National Oceanic and Atmospheric Administration, Department of Commerce, through the National Sea Grant College Program. Grant number NA86AA-D-SG006, projects M-3 and M-4.

The University of Maryland is an equal opportunity employer.

PREFACE

For decades concern has mounted over the health of the Chesapeake Bay, historically the world's richest estuary. Extensive studies by state and federal agencies reveal increasing problems resulting primarily from heavy use of the Chesapeake watershed, where population has grown from an estimated 34,000 in 1700 to some 300,000 in 1800 to almost 13 million by 1980. In these pages, J.R. Schubel, who directs the Marine Sciences Research Center, State University of New York in Stony Brook, puts the Bay's health, its life, and its inevitable death into a broad perspective. That perspective focuses not only on the geologic past of the Bay but also on the factors — physical, biological, social — that will shape its future.

Schubel — who draws on knowledge born of years of Bay research at the Johns Hopkins University Chesapeake Bay Institute — recounts in the first section the geologic history of the Chesapeake, providing a large canvas for his later discussion of Bay health and productivity. Much of this section parallels a similar discussion in his well-known book, *The Living Chesapeake*, published by the Johns Hopkins University Press.

The second section places the Chesapeake in proper relation to other estuaries around the globe. While the Bay ranks as the longest estuary in the world, Schubel reminds us that its drainage basin and sediment loads are by no means impressive in the company of many of the world's great rivers, such as China's Yellow and Yangtze.

Some readers will want to turn directly to the third section, where Schubel discusses Bay management and, perhaps unavoidably, politics. When he writes that "estuaries are the most complex segments of the entire world ocean," he is referring not only to ecological but also to social and legal complexity.

The Life and Death of the Chesapeake Bay, adapted from the Maryland Sea Grant/Marine-Estuarine-Environmental Science Lecture delivered by Schubel at the University of Maryland in the autumn of 1984, represents the inaugural volume in a new series published by the Maryland Sea Grant College, entitled "Marine Perspectives." This series of papers and books addresses issues and topics of concern related to marine management, science, and ecology. Views presented in the "Marine Perspectives" series, offered as contributions to the continuing discussion of marine affairs, are those of the respective authors and do not reflect the opinions of the University of Maryland or of the Sea Grant College Program.

Jack Greer
Editor

CONTENTS

MOSTLY BEGINNINGS AND ENDS

Robert Frost wrote, "You're searching, Joe, for things that don't exist. I mean beginnings. Ends and beginnings — there are no such things. There are only middles." For estuaries it seems like there are mostly beginnings and ends; their middles are so short. The Chesapeake Bay has had an unusually long "middle." It is atypical. The Crown Jewel, the Queen . . . whatever her title, the Chesapeake Bay will have a long reign as an estuary. There is no doubt about that. The $64,000 question is: How closely will her biologically and recreationally useful life span match her geological life span? Her geological life span will be determined by nature, although man could play a role through the so-called "greenhouse effect," caused by increasing carbon dioxide in the atmosphere. The Bay's biologically and recreationally useful life span will be determined by society . . . by us. Society will determine, then, how closely her two life spans will match — whether she will retain a quality of life for as long as she lives.

Here, I want to talk a little about life and death — and about the quality of life of the Chesapeake Bay, and her siblings and her ancestors.

And I want to do more than that. I want to look farther back and farther ahead in time, focusing on things we might do to ensure the quality of the Bay's life, recommendations for preventive environmental medicine.

Let's pause for a definition. The Bay is an *estuary* so we had best agree on what we mean by that term. The late Hugo Fisher once remarked that an estuary is a little like pornography — hard to define but you know it when you see it. Perhaps, but just as with pornography some in our society take a more liberal, a more tolerant, view of what constitutes an estuary than others. And this lack of precision in terminology has led to confusion and to an incorrect assessment of the permanence and the importance of estuaries. The definition I shall use is from D.W. Pritchard: "An estuary is a semi-enclosed coastal body of water which has a free connection with the ocean and within which sea water is measurably diluted with freshwater from land drainage." And the largest estuary, so defined, in the United States is the Chesapeake Bay.

Origin of the Modern Chesapeake Bay

The modern Chesapeake Bay is very young geologically — less than 10,000 years old. Like all of the world's other estuaries, it had its origins in the most recent rise in sea level which began 15,000 to 18,000 years ago.

At that time great ice sheets covered extensive continental areas and sea level was 100 to 125 meters below its present position. The oceans had retracted almost entirely into their oceanic basins; most of the continental shelves of the world were high and dry. The continental shelf off the middle Atlantic states is a broad, sandy plain which slopes seaward at only about 02 minutes of arc: a change in elevation of about 1 foot in 1500. Eighteen thousand years ago the shelf was covered with lush vegetation: meadows, freshwater marshes, and climax forests of boreal conifers, hemlock and northern hardwoods — trees that today are abundant only in much higher latitudes.

Ancient elephants — mastodons and mammoths — bison, musk oxen, horses and tapir roamed over a region which in only a few thousand years would be submerged deep beneath the Atlantic

Ocean. Fossil elephant bones and teeth, dredged occasionally by fishermen from the continental shelf between George's Bank and the mouth of the Chesapeake Bay, are the only reminders that those magnificent beasts once trod through forests and meadows where fish now swim.

Man probably had not arrived in this area 15,000-18,000 years ago, but he would come soon to hunt and to fish on the continental shelf. Stream valleys deeply dissected the rolling hills of the Eastern Shore, and the Susquehanna had completed carving the valley that was to receive and hold the Chesapeake Bay estuary. The scene was set for a change.

First, the climate began to warm up. The great continental ice sheets lost more to meltwater than they gained from fresh snow the winter before. Their long retreat had begun, a retreat that would continue up to the present, and perhaps longer. The meltwater was returned to the sea; and the sea, getting back its own, responded. It began to rise.

By 15,000 years ago, the sea had climbed out of its oceanic basin and begun its relentless march across the continental shelf to reclaim its territory from mastodons and conifers, to return it to fish and plankton. That march would not stop until our present shores had been reached and, perhaps, not even then.

Ecclesiastes 1:7 tells us that "All streams run to the sea, but the sea is not full." Ecclesiastes does not really apply in this case. All the streams ran to the sea, but this time the sea not only was full, it was overflowing. It spilled out of its oceanic basins and well up onto the continental blocks. Geologists call such attacks of the sea on the land "transgressions," as if to suggest that the sea has an obligation to stay within its own oceanic basin — the place it probably has stayed for nearly 90 percent of the time for the past several million years.

The rates of vertical rise and lateral advance of the sea were dramatic, not just by geological standards, but to human perceptions as well. For the first few centuries of sea level rise, the sea rose at a rate of about 5 meters per century. It then slowed, and for most of the rest of the time from 15,000 to 5,000 years ago it rose at a rate of about 1 meter per century. For every meter it rose vertically, it advanced laterally more than 1500 meters. That's equivalent to a shore erosion rate of 15 meters per year: 50 feet per year. Waterfront property would have been an even more perilous investment from 15,000 to 5,000 years ago than today. If your camp was not shorefront, it soon would be — just before it was drowned. From the time man first arrived in this region, he has been fleeing the sea. He still is.

The transgressing sea moved up the valley incised into the continental shelf by the Susquehanna, pushing back the reluctant river as it came. The river was forced to retreat toward the land and its fresh water had to move up and over the encroaching sea water. Quickly the swelling sea filled the valley, spilled out over its steep walls and flowed out onto the gentle sandy plain, inundating fresh water marshes, meadows and woodlands.

Here's the countdown:

Ten thousand years ago. The advancing sea had reached the present mouth of Chesapeake Bay. The sea continued to rise, penetrating farther and farther into the basin carved by the Susquehanna and its tributary rivers. The head of the Bay — the head of the estuary which is marked by the upstream limit of sea salt penetration — crept farther and farther inland. Eight thousand years ago the head of the Bay had reached Smith Island; 5,000 years ago Annapolis; 3,000 years ago Betterton at the mouth of the Sassafras. Then, the rate of sea level rise slowed appreciably.

Three thousand years ago. The modern Chesapeake Bay was nearly complete. It had stopped growing, or at least it grew so slowly that one could hardly detect it. Dotted with islands, tall trees extending to its shoreline, its drainage basin covered with lush vegetation, its tributaries free of fine sediments, clear and deep. Never again would the modern Chesapeake Bay be as grand as at that moment. It must have been a magnificent sight.

Three thousand years ago. The scene was set once again for a change. The Bay, barely completed, already felt the natural forces that one day would destroy it.

There have been other beginnings and endings; beginnings and endings of other Chesapeake Bays. To understand our own Bay, one must understand its ancestral bays — their birth, development and death, the frequency of their comings and goings. Estuaries come and go with the ebb and flow of the ice ages and for each there is a beginning — and an end.

Ancestral Chesapeake Bays

For the geologist the most recent chapter in the Earth's history covers the last several million years. It is called the Pleistocene and it is marked by alternating glacial and interglacial episodes. In the northern hemisphere great continental ice sheets have waxed and waned as the world temperature has fallen and risen. The level of the sea has risen and fallen in response to the retreats and advances of the great continental ice sheets. Rapid rises and falls of sea level of more than 100 meters have been common, and "Chesapeake Bays" have appeared and disappeared with each swing of the cycle.

A whole succession of Chesapeake Bays have been born, matured and died as the sea advanced and retreated in response to the changes in climate that caused the alternation of interglacial and glacial episodes. Each time the sea rose, a bay marched ahead of it across the continental shelf. If the rise was high enough, the bay reached well up onto the continental block, even to the position of our Bay. But not every rise was great enough to advance its bay so far. Many bays never passed the midpoint of the continental shelf. Each time the sea fell, the bay followed it on its retreat, lagging slightly as if to protest. If the sea fell so low that it dropped off the edge of the continental shelf, the attendant bay vanished, and a new bay was born on the next rise. This disappearance and re-emergence of bays has happened over and over during the several million years of the Pleistocene.

To understand our own Bay we must go back about 125,000 years, back to the Eemian Interglacial. The Eemian, a period of warm, ice-free conditions similar to our present Holocene Interglacial, was our most recent climatic analog.[1] Sea level stood close to its present position. There was a "Chesapeake Bay" then, probably one as large and as complex as our own Bay. But it was quite different in shape and probably in location as well.

The Eemian Interglacial did not last long. Its warmest period lasted for a brief 10,000 years and was followed by the abrupt onset of a cold glacial period. From 115,000 years ago to 20,000 years ago — the most recent glacial maximum — temperatures swung erratically up and down but, on the whole, dropped more than they rose. The climate deteriorated. Glaciers advanced and retreated, but gained more than they lost. The sea fell and rose in response. The bay shuffled back and forth across the shelf, sometimes advancing, sometimes retreating, but generally losing

---

[1] There probably was a brief interglacial with a high stand of sea level 35,000 years ago.

ground and finally falling into the sea only to be reborn a long time later.

Our Holocene Interglacial has lasted nearly 20,000 years. That is longer than man has lived in the middle Atlantic region and 10,000 years longer than our Chesapeake Bay estuary has existed. Previous interglacials lasted about 10,000 years each. Our Holocene Interglacial already has lasted twice as long. Interglacials like the Holocene with temperatures as warm or warmer than today have endured for less than 10 percent of the time over the past several million years. They have occurred roughly only once in every 100,000 years and each has lasted about 10,000 years. "Chesapeake Bays" have had the same rhythm of occurrence and duration. So what does the future hold for our Bay?

The Future

The origin and development of our Bay and the birth, development and death of its ancestral bays have been controlled by sea level fluctuations driven by climatic changes. The future of our Bay as a geological and oceanographic entity — as an estuary — is coupled tightly to what happens to sea level. If sea level remains nearly constant, the remaining life span of the Chesapeake Bay estuary will be about 10,000 years. Over that period it will become progressively smaller as it is filled with sediments. If sea level falls, the Bay's life span will be shortened. If sea level rises, its life span will be extended. The history of glacial and interglacial episodes throughout the Pleistocene suggests that the onset of a new glacial episode with a resulting drop in sea level is overdue. In a recent book Schneider and Londer (1984) state "left to her own devices, nature will continue to nudge the Earth toward the next ice age." But man's activities and their effect on nature may rewrite the next installment of the Earth's history.

An estimated 26 million cubic kilometers of glacial ice now covers about 10 percent of the land surface of the Earth. This ice is concentrated in the Greenland ice sheet, in the Antarctic ice sheet and in small glaciers in the Arctic and the Alps. Nearly 90 percent of the total is contained in the huge Antarctic ice sheet centered roughly on the South Pole. If all this ice were to melt, sea level would rise by approximately 70 meters. The Bay would be reunited with her sisters — with Delaware Bay, the Hudson River estuary and Long Island Sound to the north, and with Albemarle and Pamlico Sounds to the south. New York, Philadelphia, Baltimore, Washington and Richmond would be submerged. Most of the Eastern Shore would be drowned; only a few isolated peaks would remain as islands. But don't rush to unload your present waterfront property, or to invest in land in the Piedmont as future waterfront. It would take several thousand years to melt the entire mass of glacial ice. Significant rises in sea level could occur, however, over much shorter periods of time and many experts believe that these are inevitable.

The fate of this ice is linked to the Earth's temperature, which is a function of the sunlight the Earth receives, the sunlight it reflects and the long wave (infrared) radiation the atmosphere absorbs. If the Earth had no atmosphere, the incoming visible radiation received from the sun and the outgoing infrared radiation emitted by the Earth would reach a balance to yield a particular average surface temperature. But the atmosphere is there, and it acts as a filter: it transmits radiation selectively. The atmosphere transmits radiation in the visible part of the spectrum quite freely, but strongly absorbs longer wave radiation in the infrared part of the spectrum.

The atmosphere's filtering action is caused primarily by the water vapor and carbon dioxide (CO_2) it contains. Other atmospheric components which contribute to this filtering include ozone and dust. A change in the abundance, or in the mixture, of these constituents produces a change in the atmosphere's filtering efficiency, particularly for long-wave radiation. About 50 percent of the energy from the sun that arrives at the top of the Earth's atmosphere and at the Earth's surface are in the visible part of the spectrum. Most of the energy emitted by the Earth and its atmosphere, on the other hand, is long-wave radiation in the infrared. This long-wave energy is absorbed strongly by the Earth's atmosphere; it is trapped, causing an increase in the Earth's mean temperature. This phenomenon is known widely as the "greenhouse effect."[2]

Any increase in the atmospheric concentrations of CO_2, water vapor and ozone — the greenhouse gases — will increase the atmosphere's filtering efficiency for long-wave radiation, which will lead to the retention of a greater fraction of this energy by the Earth. This in turn will result in an increase of the Earth's mean temperature *so long as other climatic factors do not dominate.* Let's assume for the moment they do not. What can we expect?

Most of the anthropogenic CO_2 added to the atmosphere and to the ocean comes from the burning of fossil fuels. Deforestation accounts for only a small percentage of the observed increase in atmospheric CO_2, but the contribution resulting from this activity has increased over the past century. Since only a fraction of CO_2 emissions remain in the atmosphere, one cannot accurately predict concentrations from emission data alone.

It is clear that CO_2 levels in the atmosphere have increased and are continuing to increase. In the past 180 years concentrations of CO_2 in the atmosphere have risen approximately 30 percent, from about 260 ppm (parts per million) to 340 ppm, and further increases are predicted. The concentration of atmospheric CO_2 is expected to exceed 600 ppm by the third quarter of the next century and most experts agree that the levels of greenhouse gases will almost certainly double in the next century.

The increases in the atmospheric CO_2 are well established. The uncertainty lies in assessing the extent to which these increases will affect climate and, in turn, sea level. Increases in the

---

[2] The process is similar to what you observe when you park your car in the summer with the windows closed. The windows transmit the sun's energy, which is primarily in the visible spectrum. This radiation is absorbed by the seats, dashboard, floor — the interior of the car — and is re-emitted as long-wave radiation. Since the windows are nearly opaque to energy at these longer wave-lengths, this energy is trapped in the car and the temperature inside the car rises.

levels of CO_2 and other greenhouse gases act to increase the
Earth's average temperature. If there were no other factors at play,
a doubling of atmospheric CO_2 would increase the Earth's mean
temperature by about 1.2° C. But there are feedback mechanisms
which would result from any increase in temperature, regardless of
the cause. Any warming of the Earth would change the composi-
tion and reflectivity of the atmosphere and the reflectivity of the
Earth's surface. As temperature increases, water vapor increases,
snow melts and the reflectivity of the Earth decreases. The effect
of each of these consequences would be to amplify the initial direct
warming. Other effects of warming, such as changing cloud cover,
could either amplify or reduce the initial direct warming. Then
there is the larger, even more difficult question — what general
climatic trend is the greenhouse effect superimposed upon? The
causes of the onsets of previous glacial episodes were not linked to
anthropogenic inputs of CO_2; they occurred much too long ago.
We are not sure what nature has in store for us and just how great
society's impact will be when measured against that background
climatic signal. More about that later; we said we were going to
keep the story simple.

Taking into account, to the extent possible, the feedback
mechanisms mentioned above, the National Academy of Sciences
(1983) estimated that a doubling of present atmospheric CO_2
levels probably would increase the Earth's mean temperature by 1.5
to 4.5° C, and indicated that an increase in the lower half of this
range was more probable. Even this would represent a large total
temperature change when compared with historical temperature
changes (Table 1), and the predicted *rate* of increase is even more
significant when compared with historical rates of temperature
change.

Over the past 18,000 years the Earth's mean temperature has
increased by about 0.4° C. The rates of temperature rise associated
with these changes are 0.02° C per century for the past century.
The warming rate projected by the National Academy of Sciences
for the next century as a result of the greenhouse effect is 3 to 10
times the historical warming trend of the past century. An increase

Table 1. Variations in mean global temperature relative to today.

Time Period	Mean Global Temperature
Last 2-3 million years	No more than 2-3° C warmer than today
Last 100,000 years	No more than 1° C warmer than today
Last 1,000 years	No more than .5° C warmer than today

in the Earth's temperature of the magnitude predicted would have profound effects on vegetation, on agriculture, on rainfall and on sea level.

Any increase in the Earth's mean temperature will produce a world-wide (eustatic) rise in sea level. The rise will result from two processes: the melting of glacial ice which will increase the amount of water in the world's oceans, and the expansion of the upper ocean and the resulting decrease in density produced by warming. The magnitude of the rise in sea level is equivocal. Probably the most widely accepted estimates come from the National Academy of Sciences (1983), which predicts that the rise of sea level over the next century could total about 70 cm: 40 cm from water added by melting of ice and 30 cm from expansion of the upper ocean produced by warming. The Academy also adds that during the next several centuries there is the potential for an additional rise of sea level of 5 to 6 meters *if* the West Antarctic ice sheet dis-integrates. Were this to occur, there is the possibility of a rise of sea level of as much as 2 meters per century by the middle of the next century. The U.S. Environmental Protection Agency in 1983 forecast even larger and more rapid rises of sea level. But all of these predictions assume that the background music remains the same, and that Nature no longer calls the tune.

The factors that cause the onset and termination of glaciations are poorly understood, and there is no compelling evidence that man's activities have altered the basic underlying process which led to the onset of periodic glaciations that have characterized the last several million years of the Earth's history. The increases in atmospheric carbon dioxide are well documented; it is the effect of these increases that is uncertain. The greenhouse effect is superimposed upon a natural climatic background signal and it is unclear how it will affect the strength and the character of that signal. One can cool the car in summer, even with the windows closed, if one turns on the air conditioner.

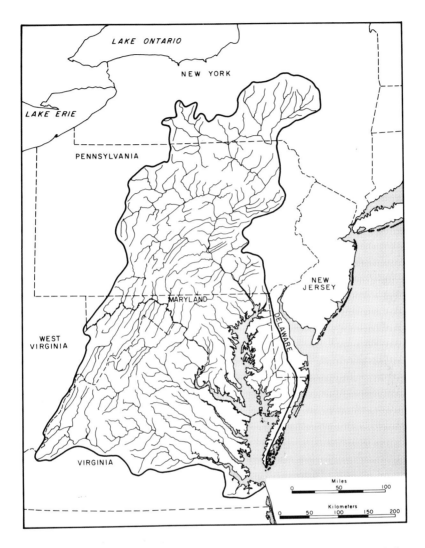

The Watershed of the Chesapeake Bay. Draining parts of six states from New York to Virginia, the Chesapeake watershed comprises a tangle of tributaries. Each stream or river funnels rain waters to the estuary from the Appalachian Mountains, the piedmont and the coastal plain.

A DOMINION
OF SALT
AND SEDIMENT

T he Bay and its tributaries are filling with sediment; they
are filling from their heads, and to a lesser extent from their
mouths. As they do, the surface area, depth, volume and inter-
tidal volume all decrease. The conduits to the sea get more
restricted. Since river flows are unaffected, they flow harder and
faster through their smaller pipes and the sea is pushed progressively seaward down the Bay and down each of its tributaries.
Eventually the Bay will be filled to the point where it will have an
estuary only during periods of low river flow. Only then will the
sea be able to poke its nose into the Bay basin.

Inevitably, the Bay will reach a stage where the river flow
will be sufficiently strong even in periods of low flow to keep the
sea from penetrating into the Bay basin. At that stage the
Chesapeake Bay estuary will have been destroyed. It will have
gone through the entire evolution: from river valley to estuary to
river valley. There still will be a river valley and there still will be
an extensive area of low salinity off the mouth of the Bay — indeed it will be larger than now — where "estuarine-dependent"
organisms could grow and reproduce, but there will no longer be

an estuary. If relative sea level remains near its present level, this process will take about 10,000 years more to complete.

The Bay system now is roughly half-filled with sediment. Again, if sea level rises, the geological life span of the Bay will be extended. If sea level falls, its life span will be abbreviated.

An Estuary in Motion

When the sea invaded the Bay valley 10,000 years ago, it triggered a series of basic and fundamental changes to the water body that makes its home within this basin, changes that made it neither river nor sea. The changes started at the mouth and were transmitted progressively up the main stem of the Bay and off into each of its tributaries as the sea rose and penetrated farther and farther into the old river valley system. The Susquehanna struggled to push the sea back out of its valley, to retain its domain, but the task was too much even for the mighty Susquehanna. It carried more water than it had when it was master of its valley, but now things were different. The stronger the Susquehanna flowed and the harder it pushed, the more the sea rose and the farther it advanced.

The assault and the retreat went on inexorably: the head of the Bay reached Smith Island 8,000 years ago, Annapolis 5,000 years ago, Betterton 3,000 years ago.

Now the Susquehanna would have to flow up and over the denser sea water to reach the open sea. The Patuxent and the Potomac, the Rappahannock and the York, the Choptank and the Chester and all the other rivers that once paid tribute to the Susquehanna, now shifted their allegiance to the sea. Even the once proud and independent James had been captured; the sea had succeeded where the Susquehanna had failed.

Where the Susquehanna had once flowed constantly to the sea now was a great bay, a bay whose surface rose and fell twice each day, rhythmically, like a giant organism inhaling and exhaling. The bay seemed almost alive and indeed it was. It teemed with life; life far more abundant and diverse than it had known before. The water no longer flowed constantly to the sea; its principal motion now was an oscillatory one. The Indians called it a river that flowed in two directions. But it is more than a river, more even than a river that flows in two directions — more than a tidal river — it is a giant mixing basin for sea water and river water. It is an estuary; the great Chesapeake Bay estuarine system — perhaps the world's most magnificent estuary, and certainly one of the largest and most productive.

To understand the struggle between river and sea we must look at the details of the action. The river flows in one direction, seaward, and its water is fresh. The minuscule amounts of salts dissolved in it have been leached from the land through which it flows and their proportions are quite different from those of the salt in the sea. Fresh water is lighter than salt water. The salinity of water is in fact a rough guide to its density; the more salt it contains, the heavier it is.

The river must get its water to the sea. There is nothing else it can do with it. More is coming all the time. Water doesn't "stack" very well, and the river has no place to store it. The river relieves itself in the only way it can. The lighter fresh water over-runs the heavier salt water and flows down the Bay to the ocean in an upper layer across a lower layer of sea water. But a number of things happen to it along the way.

One of the most potent weapons in the arsenal of the sea is the tide. Were the Bay an enclosed lake, the tides would be very small; perhaps a centimeter or so. As it is, open to the sea at the Virginia Capes, twice each day an oceanic high tide of consider-able size is delivered at its mouth by the moon and the sun which then continue on about their business. Left to its own devices the mound of water enters the Bay and rolls up its length as a free wave. The surface of the Bay rises and falls twice each day. Accompanying the succession of high and low waters are tidal currents which change direction approximately every six hours. Unlike the river, the Bay, under the governance of the sea, flows alternately in two directions: landward, then seaward, then land-ward again.

However, the power of the tide in the battle between river and sea is its power to mix. It is the egg beater that stirs up the water in the Bay. Were there no tide, a heavy torpid layer of salty water would lie in the bottom of the Bay, and over it a lighter layer of essentially fresh water would run to the sea. Because water has some internal friction — some viscosity — though not much, some sea salt would be mixed into the upper layer, but in such small amounts that the upper layer would remain potable most of the way to the Virginia Capes.

But the tide is there. The great mass of water in the Bay sloshes back and forth at speeds which reach 2 knots — 100 centimeters per second. The flows are turbulent and tear great globs from both layers. From the upper layer the globs are carried down into the lower layer, and globs from the lower layer are transferred to the upper. There they mix so that the "fresh" upper layer becomes increasingly salty toward the mouth of the Bay while the "salty" lower layer becomes increasingly fresh toward the head of the Bay, yet at any given place in the Bay the lower layer is always saltier and denser than the upper layer. The difference in salinity between the two layers is nearly the same over much of the length of the Bay (Figure 1).

The sea salt mixed into the upper layer is discharged, mixed with the fresh river water, back into the sea. If this attrition of the lower layer were to go on without compensation, the river would win a quick victory. The entire Bay would soon be "fresh" from top to bottom. The sea would have been eliminated, and the Bay would no longer be an estuary. But this has not happened. While the total inventory of salt in the system varies seasonally and, somewhat, from year to year, its average salinity has remained essentially unchanged for thousands of years. There must be a supply of salt, an inexhaustible supply. And there is: the sea. For every part of it that is driven out, it has a replacement. Compared to the Bay, the sea is infinite, its volume 20 million times greater. A slow persistent current moves silently up the Bay in the lower layer to resupply the salt that has been flushed out to sea in the upper layer.

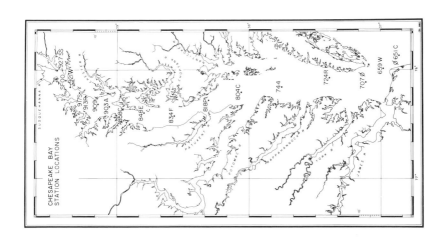

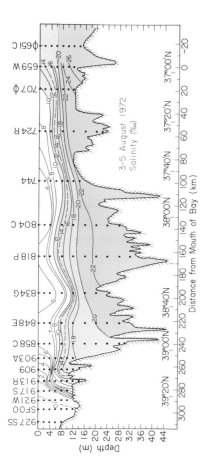

Figure 1. The Chesapeake's layers of salt. Along the length of the Chesapeake, layers of fresher water flow over heavier, more saline waters. This chart shows sampling stations, 17 in all, from some 20 miles beyond the mouth of the Bay all the way to the Elk River near the Bay's head. Though estuarine waters are saltier at the Bay's mouth, the difference in salinity between surface waters and bottom waters remains fairly constant throughout the Bay. This sampling of the Chesapeake took place in August, 1972.

We have seen that the rivers must discharge their water to the ocean. On the average, the rivers entering the Bay must get rid of about 2,000 cubic meters every second. However, when we measure the discharge to the ocean in the upper layer through the mouth of the Bay we find the discharge is not 2,000 cubic meters per second, but that it averages about 20,000 cubic meters per second, 10 times as much. This excess water is water transported from the lower layer to the upper layer by a steady vertical flow which occurs along the entire length of the estuary. This vertical motion, called the entrainment velocity, transports water and salt from the lower layer into the upper layer. Random, turbulent motions also occur. On the average, they do not produce a net transport of water but do lead to a net transport of salt from the higher salinity lower layer to the fresher upper layer.

Since the amount of water in the Bay has changed very little from week to week, from year to year, or even from century to century over at least the past several thousand years, it is clear that the flow of sea water into the Bay in the lower layer must be nine times the fresh water flow of all the rivers that enter it. The net difference in the flows of the two layers through the Capes must equal the total fresh water input to the Bay; no more, no less, if the volume of the Bay is to be maintained. Since the total fresh water input to the Bay varies seasonally and from year to year, the total net discharge through the mouth of the Bay also changes, but not by a great deal. The ratio of the discharge of the upper layer to the fresh water input also varies seasonally and from year to year, but roughly inversely to the variation in fresh water input. As a result, the volume rate of outflow of the upper layer does not vary greatly.

We have, then, the oscillatory tidal flow which is the dominant circulation pattern in the Bay. Part of the potential energy of this highly organized, periodic flow is dissipated through the kinetic energy of the highly disorganized, aperiodic, random turbulent motions which mix fresh water and sea water. The resulting density field drives a second highly organized flow pattern — estuarine circulation (Figure 2). It is this slower, more subtle circulation that moves water persistently seaward in the upper layer and landward in the lower layer — at speeds of only about one-fifth those of the stronger tidal currents — that is in many respects the more important circulation pattern. We observe these kinds of circulation patterns not only in the Bay proper, but in each of its larger tributary estuaries.

We have then the oscillatory tidal circulation with speeds of up to 100 centimeters per second, the vertical circulation with speeds of up to about 0.001 centimeters per second, and the estuarine circulation with speeds which average about 5 to 10 centimeters per second.

Our sketch of the arena is almost complete except that we have not mentioned that the struggle between river and sea takes place on a carousel: the Earth rotates. As a result of this rotation in the northern hemisphere every motion is deflected to its right. The upper seaward-flowing layer is bent toward the western shore of the Bay while the lower landward-flowing layer is bent toward the Eastern Shore. The upper layer is thicker to the west and the lower layer thicker to the east. The division between them is thus not level. It slopes upward to the east (Figure 3). As a result, along any horizontal east-west line across the Bay salinity increases eastward and the water is saltier along the Eastern Shore.

The fluctuating force of the Susquehanna constantly plays against the encroaching sea; the fresh water, driven by gravity, presses against the leading edge of the invading sea water. When the river is in spate, it forces the sea to retreat. When river flow decreases the sea rebounds, advancing quickly to reclaim its territory. So the skirmish line sways back and forth with the seasons. The Susquehanna runs most strongly in late winter and early spring, when water that has been locked up in snow and ice over much of Pennsylvania and New York is suddenly freed to add to the warm spring rains that feed it. The sea retreats nearly to Tolchester, across from the present-day Patapsco. Summer drought robs the river of munitions and permits the sea, albeit a diluted one, to advance to Turkey Point at the head of the Bay and beyond. In late fall rains once again bring a lesser renewal of fresh

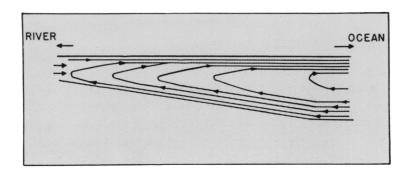

Figure 2. The Bay's circulating machine. Swinging in great curves, salt water from the sea enters the estuary along the Bay floor then turns back, dragged by the rivers' fresh water. This is the typical circulation pattern in a partially mixed estuary such as the Chesapeake Bay. In the actual estuary, these smooth lines break into eddies and pockets of fresh water, mixed with the salt.

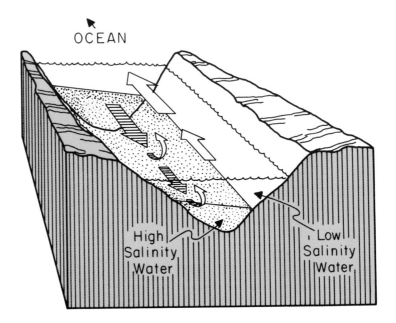

Figure 3. A slanted saline boundary. Because of the earth's rotation, heavier, saltier waters are deflected toward the east, while southward flowing fresh waters are deflected toward the west. The cause of this deflection is the so-called Coriolis effect. The result is a tilted boundary between Bay bottom waters and fresher surface waters.

water and the sea again retreats, only to advance once more as winter locks up the water throughout the drainage basin of the Susquehanna. Once in a while the river finds an ally in a tropical storm. In June, 1972, Tropical Storm Agnes gave the Susquehanna enough ammunition to drive the sea all the way back to Annapolis, farther seaward than had ever been recorded.

An impressive assault by the Susquehanna; but even with a riverflow of a magnitude it could muster only once in every two hundred years, the Susquehanna could not drive the sea back by even 20% of its total penetration. For now, the Susquehanna and her sisters will have to be patient and bide their time. The sea will prove to be a more persistent and tenacious adversary for them than the soft Coastal Plain sediments they eroded to produce this expansive river valley system many thousands of years ago. Then they had done their work too well, and now they would pay the price. If only the valley system were not so large, the sea would not be such a formidable foe. As it is, the sea will remain in the Bay basin long after it has been expelled from most other semi-enclosed coastal basins around the world. The Chesapeake Bay estuary will outlive almost all of her sisters, but what will the quality of her life be? Before turning to that topic, let's briefly examine the Chesapeake Bay's standing in the community of estuaries.

In the Community of Estuaries

All of the present members of the world's community of estuaries are roughly the same age. All were formed during the most recent rise in sea level and all are less than 10,000 years old. All, as my sister-in-law would say when asked about her age relative to that of other women, are contemporaries. But the Chesapeake Bay is anomalous among them. It is larger than most and, relative to its volume, receives a smaller input of sediment than most. We can find estuaries around the world in various stages of geological evolution: some, like the Chesapeake Bay and Long Island Sound, are immature and largely unfilled. Others like the Atchafalaya in

Louisiana and the Huang Ho (Yellow) in China have been filled completely and are now essentially rivers without estuaries. Still others like the Changjiang (Yangtze) in China, which only a few thousand years ago had a large magnificent estuary, now have an estuary only during periods of low river discharge. Only then is the force of the river too weak to keep the sea out of what remains of its semi-enclosed coastal basin. Table 2 compares the sizes (lengths) of some of the world's major estuaries at low and high river discharges. The Chesapeake Bay is the largest — the longest — estuary at all stages of river flow.

A quick comparison of the sediment discharges of the Changjiang (Yangtze), the Huang Ho (Yellow) and the Susquehanna is instructive in understanding the Bay's youthful stage of development. The long-term average discharge of sediment by the

Table 2. Lengths of some of the world's estuaries during periods of high river flow and low river flow. (The length of the estuary is defined as the distance from the mouth of the estuarine basin at its seaward end inland to the last traces of measurable sea salt.)

Estuary	Country	Length in km at High River flow	Length in km at Low River flow
Amazon	Brazil	0	0
Changjiang (Yangtze)	China	0–10	30–40
Chesapeake Bay	*USA*	*280*	*320*
Congo	Zaire	0–5	40
Huang Ho (Yellow)	China	0	0
Hudson	USA	25	55
Long Island Sound	USA	145	150
Mississippi	USA	10	100
Rio de la Plata	Argentina	150	300
San Francisco Bay	USA	50	60
St. Lawrence	Canada	150	175

Susquehanna is about one million tons per year. All the other rivers tributary to the Bay might triple the amount of river-borne sediment discharged into the Chesapeake Bay system. By contrast, the Changjiang discharges about 500 million tons of sediment per year and the Huang Ho about one billion tons per year. By seven o'clock every evening of every day, the Changjiang has discharged as much sediment as the Susquehanna will in an entire year. The Huang Ho accomplishes this task before breakfast at nine every morning of every day.

There is another way of looking at this. The Chesapeake Bay, the Huang Ho estuary and the Changjiang estuary all were formed at the same time. The Huang Ho estuary received as much sediment in its first ten years of existence as the Chesapeake Bay has from the Susquehanna over its entire life span of 10,000 years as an estuary. The somewhat less impressive Changjiang took 20 years to accomplish the same task.

The top ten rivers of the world ranked by their discharges of suspended sediment are listed in Table 3. The Susquehanna is not among them. The sediment discharge of the last river on the list exceeds that of the Susquehanna by 160 times.

The area and volume of the Bay are enormous compared with most other estuaries, though its sediment inputs are puny. The Bay has a relatively large drainage area which includes parts of six states — Pennsylvania, New York, Maryland, Delaware, West Virginia and Virginia — and it is the receiving waters for more than 150 rivers and creeks, 50 of which are considered major. This is the principal challenge facing those who manage the Bay and who seek to conserve its multi-use character. Most of the Bay's most serious problems are inherited from its tributaries; they are dumped on it, or in it, if you will. The population in the Bay's drainage basin increased by more than 4.2 million between 1950 and 1980 and is expected to grow an additional 1.9 million to a total of 14.5 million by the year 2000.

Before we begin to feel too sorry for ourselves, it might be useful to put the Bay's drainage basin and the population that resides within that drainage basin in perspective. Consider the

Table 3. Rivers of the world ranked by suspended sediment discharge.

Rank	River	Country	Average Suspended Sediment Discharge at the *River's* Mouth in Millions of Metric Tons per Year
1	Ganges-Brahmputra	Bangladesh	1670
2	Huang Ho (Yellow)	China	1080
3	Amazon	Brazil	900
4	Changjiang (Yangtze)	China	500
5	Irrawaddy	Burma	285
6	Magdalena	Colombia	210
7	Mississippi (including Atchafalaya)	USA	220
8	Orinoco	Venezuela	160
9	Mekong	S. Vietnam	160
10	Red	USA	160
—	*Susquehanna*	USA	1

Mississippi and the Changjiang estuaries. The Mississippi has a drainage area of some 3,225,000 square kilometers — nearly 20 times that of the Chesapeake — and the Changjiang's drainage basin of 1,950,000 square kilometers is nearly 12 times that of the Chesapeake Bay's 165,760 square kilometers. The ten largest rivers in the world in terms of drainage areas are summarized in Table 4, along with the entire Chesapeake Bay estuarine system.

More people live within the drainage basin of the Changjiang estuary than within the drainage basin of any other estuary in the world. The total population in its drainage basin not only exceeds that of the Chesapeake Bay, but of the Chesapeake Bay plus the

Table 4. Rivers of the world ranked by area of drainage basin for comparison with the drainage basin of the entire Chesapeake Bay estuarine systems.

Rank	River	Country	Drainage Area in Thousands of Square Kilometers
1	Amazon	Brazil	5,775
2	Congo	Zaire	4,025
3	Mississippi	USA and Canada	3,225
4	Nile	Egypt	2,975
5	Yenisei	USSR	2,600
6	Ob	USSR	2,500
7	Lena	USSR	2,425
8	Parana	Argentina	2,300
9	Changjiang	China	1,950
10	Amur	USSR	1,850
—	*Chesapeake Bay*	*USA*	166[3]

Mississippi; and indeed of the Chesapeake plus the Mississippi plus the populations of all the 850 estuaries in the entire United States combined: more than five times as many. A total of 400 to 500 million people live within the drainage basin of the Changjiang — more than 30 times as many as within the drainage basin of the Chesapeake Bay.

---

[3] The drainage basin of the entire Chesapeake Bay estuarine system is 165,700 square kilometers.

RETAINING A
QUALITY OF LIFE

When John Adams, a Democrat, was President, he wrote in his diary that he swam in the upper Potomac near Washington, D.C. When Lincoln, a Republican, became President he wrote in his diary that not only did he not swim in the upper Potomac, but that on warm humid summer evenings when the wind was off the Potomac the stench sometimes was so bad that he and his family had to flee the White House. There are at least two possible interpretations for this difference in behavior of these two presidents. The most obvious is that it indicates that the water quality of the upper Potomac was degraded severely over this period of approximately 60 years. (The second interpretation, the one I suspect Ronald Reagan would give you if he were here today, is that it indicates only that "a Democrat will swim in anything.")

Reclaiming the Chesapeake Bay

If water quality has declined in the Chesapeake, what have been the signals of distress?

• Harvests of freshwater-spawning fish have been declining for a decade. Among them are striped bass, perch and shad.

• Harvests of oysters have declined Bay-wide and there has been only one good set of spat in the last decade.

• Submerged aquatic vegetation has declined in diversity and in abundance since the late 1960s; the losses are particularly extensive in the upper Bay.

• Blooms of blue-green algae and dinoflagellates have been occurring in the upper Bay with increasing frequency in recent years, replacing more desirable species. According to the EPA's Chesapeake Bay Program, counts of these organisms have increased about 250-fold since the 1950s.

• Levels of nutrients are increasing in many parts of the Bay.

• The zone of low oxygen — a natural feature of the Chesapeake Bay — has increased in extent and in duration. The phenomenon is not new, but it appears to have been exacerbated. The zone of low oxygen now covers a larger area and volume of the Bay — the EPA says the volume has increased 15-fold since 1950. It appears earlier in the year and persists later in the autumn. It is a symptom of a chronic problem that is increasing in severity — over-enrichment of the Bay with nutrients, nutrients from incompletely treated domestic sewage, from agricultural runoff and from animal wastes. This continues to be the Bay's most serious problem.

These and many of the Bay's other serious pollution and management problems are related to the Bay's estuarine circulation, which entraps not only sediment but particle-associated contaminants and dissolved constituents as well. The Bay's waters, which total some 27 billion cubic meters, are continuously renewed with salt water from the ocean and fresh water from its rivers. The Bay receives an average of approximately 2,000 cubic meters of new fresh water every second; more in spring when river flow is high, less in summer when river flow is low. Throughout the Bay, this fresh water is mixed with sea water that enters through its mouth at the Virginia Capes and is discharged seaward. The length of time the average water molecule spends in the Bay is about six months. This is equivalent to saying that the entire volume of the Bay is replenished about twice a year.

The waters that flow into the Bay carry in solution every natural element listed in the periodic table along with a long list of anthropogenic substances. The waters also carry particles in suspension — fine-grained organic and inorganic sedimentary particles and substances which these particles carry adsorbed to their surfaces. Long after the waters that carried them in have left the Bay, the particles and the constituents adsorbed to their surfaces are still to be found. They are trapped. The actions of the Bay which remove and retain — which filter out — materials in suspension and in solution result primarily from its estuarine circulation.

This filtering action has important practical as well as scientific implications. It leads, or at least contributes in a substantial way, to many of the Bay's most serious pollution and management problems, mentioned above: the accumulation of contaminants in sediments; dredging and dredged material disposal, particularly of contaminated sediments; nutrient enrichment; dissolved oxygen depletion; degradation and loss of benthic habitat; loss of submerged aquatic vegetation; and many others.

The Bay's filtering processes also have an ameliorative side; they contribute to improved estuarine water quality. Despite high loadings of nutrients and contaminants, fine particles suspended within the water column scavenge dissolved and colloidal substances, scrub them from the water column and transfer them to the bottom of the Bay. Some are retained there quasi-permanently; others, such as nutrients, are not bound so tightly and leak back into the overlying waters, promoting the recycling of nutrients which sustains a high rate of primary production. This too is desirable — up to a point — because it contributes to a high secondary production of finfish and shellfish. But there is a threshold which we have exceeded in the upper reaches of the main body of the Bay and in the upper reaches of many of its tributaries, and the zone of over-enrichment is encroaching progressively farther into the Bay.

Ernest L. Wynder (M.D.) once remarked that: "It should be a function of medicine to have people die young as late as possible." It should be a function, perhaps the primary function, of estuarine management, a branch of environmental medicine, to do everything possible to ensure that the Bay's productive life span matches as closely as possible its geological life span; that it retains a quality of life so long as it lives. I prefer to think of the Bay's "quality" in terms of its capacity to fulfill the uses which we as a society wish to make of it. If that sounds anthropocentric, forgive me, but the Bay's principal importance — like that of every other estuary — is to society. The life spans of estuaries are too short, their frequencies of occurrence too low to make them very important in the larger ecological and geochemical schemes. But their importance to us is enormous, and they deserve our concerted and considered (that is, reached after deliberation and careful thought) attention.

Limitations of Current Management Programs

Since enormous amounts of money have been spent on "doctoring the Chesapeake Bay" — probably approaching $100,000,000 over the past decade — why is the patient doing so badly? Is it perhaps beyond saving — despite all the bumper stickers? Is it perhaps time to follow that old admonition, "Die and be done with it?" Should we perhaps mark the Bay's passing by borrowing the following inscription from a Connecticut tombstone: "She lived for better or worse, but died for good"? I think not. But if we want to improve our success in rehabilitating the patient and in keeping her well, we will have to change the ways in which we approach her problems.

Over the past quarter of a century — and perhaps longer — the Bay hasn't developed any new exotic diseases; to be sure there are some new chemicals in her bloodstream that she doesn't know how to deal with because she's never seen them before. But by and large she has the same set of problems she had in 1950. D.W. Pritchard's diagnosis, around 1960, put improperly treated sewage and municipal wastes at the top of the list. My own diagnosis in 1971 came to the same conclusion. I wrote then, "At the present time, sewage, pesticides, herbicides and heavy metals pose the Chesapeake Bay's greatest threats." In that same document Pritchard wrote, "It is my opinion that the most serious pollution problem in the Chesapeake Bay and its tributary tidal waterways from the standpoint of existing and future restrictions on human use of these waters for harvest of living resources and for all recreational uses including the enjoyment of an aesthetically pleasing natural surrounding is the discharge of partially treated domestic sewage."

The Bay's future as a viable, multi-use resource rests squarely in our hands. The problems are complex and are not amenable to facile solutions. One lesson we learned from the U.S. Environmental Protection Agency's Chesapeake Bay Program was that directing large sums of money to an intensive attack on a problem guarantees neither that it will lead to improvement of our understanding of the underlying causes of that problem, nor that it will lead to effective ways of dealing with it.

Because of the enormous importance of the Bay to society and because of the increasingly beleaguered and stressed nature of much of it, it is not surprising that society has demanded that government direct its attention to protecting and, when necessary, to rehabilitating this valuable natural resource. It also is not surprising that our attention has been directed at developing strategies to stop pollutants and pollution and to enhance aesthetic values and living resources. The responses of our elected officials at all levels to citizens' demands for action and the programs generated by our Federal and State agencies responsible for protecting and managing the Bay are laudable. One cannot argue with their intent. But there is a problem. The programs have not worked. They have been only marginally effective and efficient in improving our scientific understanding of the Bay and in improving our ability to manage it. These two activities — the generation of new

knowledge and our ability to apply it — are closely coupled. I
think we have lost sight of the sequence that is required for
effective management.

Estuaries probably are the most complex segments of the
entire world ocean. They certainly are the most variable.
Characteristic properties which change on time scales of hours in
estuaries change by comparable amounts in the open ocean only
over periods of years, or even decades and in some cases centuries.
And spatially these same properties can change in estuaries over
distances of a few meters in the vertical and a few kilometers in
the horizontal, where in the open ocean changes of the same

magnitude occur only over distances of tens to hundreds of meters in the vertical and thousands to tens of thousands of kilometers in the horizontal. There is a further complication in estuaries. In many estuaries man has compounded to a significant degree the already complex interactions of natural processes. Human activities have modified natural processes in estuaries in ways and to degrees that are wrought by Nature in the open ocean only over geologic time spans.

When one examines estuarine research — and Chesapeake Bay research is a paradigm — within the broader context of marine research, several striking differences emerge. In open ocean research, there is a healthy competition for funds from individual scientists and marine institutions throughout the country and indeed the world. This competition ensures a sustained high level of scientific creativity and productivity. By contrast, coastal areas, particularly estuaries, are considered to be the turf of the scientists and the institutions which reside in the states bordering each particular water body. This parochial approach to estuarine science has had unfortunate consequences.

The open ocean model is not entirely applicable to estuarine and nearshore studies, but there are some valuable lessons to be learned. In the open ocean the research that is conducted is determined in large measure by the scientific community — by the quality of their ideas and the scientific persuasion of their arguments. The scientists determine what scientific questions should be pursued and how they should be attacked. The priorities emerge out of the well-developed peer review process. As one approaches the coastline, socio-political factors play an increasingly larger role in determining what scientific questions should be pursued, how they should be addressed, and whether or not specific research will be funded. Within estuaries the socio-political factors dominate. This is not surprising in view of the enormous importance of estuaries to society, the multiple and conflicting uses we make of them, the variety of political jurisdictions, and the degradation of many of our estuaries that has resulted from these conflicting demands. Once again the Chesapeake Bay is a paradigm of this degradation. The pressure has been to develop applied pro-grams, relevant programs, responsive programs — and the pressure has been intense. Note the EPA's Chesapeake Bay Program.

It is appropriate that citizens through the political process should determine our objectives in using our environment — in-cluding the Chesapeake Bay and other estuaries. These objectives dictate the kinds of management strategies needed to ensure the coexistence of multiple and conflicting uses. It follows that it is appropriate for citizens, through citizens' advisory groups and other public participation mechanisms, to play a leadership role in de-fining management objectives and goals. What I find distressing and inappropriate is to transfer the responsibility for sophisticated scientific and technical decisions necessary to attain those objectives into the hands of concerned, well-intentioned people who lack the scientific and technical training needed to make sound scientific judgements. We have confused and confounded social problems and scientific problems.

Public decisions about how to use our environment are quite different from decisions about what science should be conducted to permit the development of management strategies to accommodate those uses. Science if done properly will allow us to understand our environment better and will enable us to predict with greater certainty how proposed uses will affect the environment. The results of these scientific investigations will allow the broader community to make choices which will have predictable and acceptable consequences. When these two roles are intertwined neither science nor society is well served. This is precisely what has happened in our dealings with estuaries. As Lewis Thomas has observed, "There are some things about which it is not true to say that every man has a right to his own opinion." Too often opinions by people who lack scientific or technical expertise have determined scientific programs and technical policies for the Bay and for other estuaries. This trend is increasing.

Because of the lack of an appropriate foundation for our understanding of the Bay and processes which characterize it, the typical management solution to a practical problem is an ad hoc attack on an unexpected problem — sometimes resulting in an even larger surprise, but more often simply failing to yield the desired result.

Because of the nature of the Bay and other estuarine systems, their importance extends well beyond the boundaries of the states which border them, often to the entire nation. Because many of their most serious problems result from activities throughout their drainage basins, it is appropriate that the Federal government should enter into partnerships with the states to fund research and monitoring activities to improve our understanding of estuaries, and to fund development and implementation of management strategies to conserve and, when necessary, to rehabilitate these important natural resources.

The partnerships which have been formed between the Federal government and the states have been primarily with state environmental management agencies. These agencies often have used the funds provided to build up large in-house staffs. On the surface, this strategy might seem desirable. It provides the states with staff committed to the problems of concern, people who do not have the distractions of graduate students and other commitments that normally go along with the responsibilities of academic scientists. But several serious problems arise in the short term and in the longer term from this strategy.

First, state agencies and, as a result, state staff are under enormous pressure to produce quick payoffs, to do "relevant" research on environmental problems currently in the news, and to apply the results of that research quickly — often before there is an adequate basis for its application. Governmental agencies are subject to shifting socio-political winds, and environmental priorities follow. Often it is impossible for governmental scientists to stay with a problem long enough to resolve it.

Academic scientists often play only minor roles in these partnerships. If they are involved at all, it often is through response to RFPs which are written by program directors who are not estuarine scientists and which typically are so over-specified as to stifle creativity and innovation and to discourage the best scientists from applying. Academic scientists find themselves in the position of competing for funds to do estuarine research which has been developed by others, who often are much less qualified. The net result of the process is that academic scientists, particularly many of the better ones, have been alienated and many have shifted their professional allegiances away from the estuary to less political realms of the environment — either farther downstream or farther upstream.

There is a further, longer-term problem. The short-term gains in responsiveness of a large in-house staff over time is transformed into a substantial loss in the states' ability to respond effectively to a changing mix of scientific and technical problems. The mix of problems changes, but the technical competencies of the civil service staffs are unable to adapt to these changes. The states develop large payrolls which must be met and they become increasingly more reluctant to divert funds to scientists outside the organizations who are equipped to attack these new problems effectively. State scientists find themselves doing research for which they are ill-equipped and the states lose the flexibility to match problems with the best problem solvers regardless of their affiliations. Both estuarine science and society are losers.

Of the existing mechanisms for Federal-state partnerships to fund research in estuaries, the one which I believe has been most effective in stimulating high-quality estuarine research is the National Sea Grant College Program. Sea Grant has been responsive to management, has been successful in attracting good researchers, and has been successful in translating the results of that research into forms usable by environmental managers. If the Sea Grant mechanism were to be used on a larger scale, for multi-year, multi-institutional, interdisciplinary studies, some changes in program design and administration would be desirable. Such expansion would require extension of intra-state Sea Grant review panels to include specialists from outside the state and, for many estuaries, more active and coordinated cooperation between two or more different Sea Grant Programs. And the annual Sea Grant funeral dance would have to be eliminated: annual threats to the continuation of this important program have been debilitating.

Because estuaries and estuarine ecosystems are particularly vulnerable to events — both natural, such as floods and hurricanes, and man-made, such as large accidental spills — special contingency funds should be established to provide rapid funding to take full advantage of the unusual scientific opportunities these "experiments" offer scientists. Documentation of the effects of events can offer valuable insights to scientists and managers into how estuaries respond to natural and anthropogenic stresses. Conventional funding mechanisms cannot respond on appropriate time scales for studies of events. The extensive studies of the effects of Tropical Storm Agnes (June 1972) on the Chesapeake Bay were possible because of the foresight and the courage of the Directors of the Johns Hopkins Chesapeake Bay Institute, the University of Maryland Chesapeake Biological Laboratory and William and Mary's Virginia Institute of Marine Sciences. Studies were started within two days of peak flooding and continued for weeks before even unofficial commitments of support were secured.

More money for estuarine research is not the answer, not alone. While more research support may well be needed and justifiable, if it is not preceded or accompanied by fundamental structural (organizational) changes in the ways in which estuarine programs are designed and conducted, we should expect to see only marginal improvement in our understanding of estuaries and in our ability to manage them effectively.

While more money alone is not the answer, neither are more of the same kinds of studies which we have conducted in the past. "Good" estuarine research must be programmatic. Not only must the individual pieces — the projects — be good, but they must fit into larger, carefully conceived, scientifically sound, interdisciplinary programs. Each estuary is unique in its totality, but there are primary characteristics shared by all which permit judicious transfer of at least some of what is learned in one estuary to some or all of the others. The processes acting in all estuaries are the same, but the relative importance of those processes, their

interactions and the manifestations of those interactions, vary sub-
stantially not only from one estuary to the next, but in different
segments of any given estuary at any given time. In addition, there
are large temporal variations in estuarine processes and in the
characteristic properties produced by those processes. The programs
must be designed to permit us to understand how individual estuarine systems operate. It is this level of understanding — of
specific estuarine *systems* — that is required for the development of
effective management strategies.

Many of the most important first-order disciplinary scientific
questions in estuaries have been addressed; few of the second-order
disciplinary questions have been considered; and almost none of the
most important, complex interdisciplinary questions that relate to
the interactions of the physical, chemical, biological and geological
processes have been studied. It is this level of understanding which
is required for effective management. The most important estuarine
questions — at least for management — are fundamentally interdisciplinary in character.

This level of understanding, which effective management
requires, is also the level which discourages funding from organizations, such as the National Science Foundation, that support
fundamental research. The next generation of scientific questions
will be enormously more difficult than the first, but it is on the
first where most scientists make their reputations.

The second order questions are complex and are not amenable to facile solutions or to attack by large, short-term (three- to
five-year) efforts. Basic research on complex estuarine interactions
cannot yet provide an adequate scientific basis for effective management of estuarine systems.

To manage estuaries *effectively* we need predictive models —
models which are both process-oriented (causal) and empirically
based. On balance, our modeling efforts to date have been useful,
but they may well have outrun our understanding of the processes
upon which they are based. Many unwary citizens and environmental managers are prone to place blind faith in the output of
computers and models. I would remind you of T.H. Huxley's

admonition in 1869 to the Geological Society of London regarding premature extrapolations from mathematical treatment to biological problems. "This seems to be one of the many cases in which the admitted accuracy of mathematical processes is allowed to throw a wholly inadmissible appearance of authority over the results obtained by them . . . . As the grandest mill in the world will not extract wheat flour from peascods, so pages of formulas will not get a definite result out of loose data."

The most important estuarine studies, then, are comprehensive, multi-year interdisciplinary studies of entire estuarine systems. Such studies fare poorly in competition for funds at the National Science Foundation. Interdisciplinary studies often "fall through the cracks" at NSF, since there is no longer any interdisciplinary program. And regional studies are frowned upon.

Continental shelf studies, on the other hand, are in an explosive stage of development. While present funding is insufficient to support all of the excellent studies being proposed, the science is sufficiently exciting that it is attracting increasingly the attention of many excellent marine scientists as well as drawing people from other disciplines, such as applied mathematics. The situation in estuaries is the reverse. Some of the best scientists who worked formerly in estuaries are directing their attention farther seaward where projects are judged on their scientific merits and not on their political desirability.

Most of the contributions to the refereed literature on estuaries have been produced by academic scientists. While this is only one measure of scientific productivity, and an imperfect one at that, it does provide some useful information. C.B. Officer and others in 1981 analyzed the institutional affiliations of senior authors of refereed papers and the identifiable Federal funding of estuarine research. They reported that over a five-year period, 1975-1980, the academic community produced 77 percent of the refereed publications, followed by Federal laboratories (15 percent) and state, municipal, industrial and other sources (8 percent). An analysis of Federal funding related to ocean pollution research, development and monitoring showed that the projects in fiscal year

1978 were funded at a total of $164 million, of which $131 million was ascribed to research, including $40.6 million related to estuaries (Interagency Committee on Ocean Pollution Research, Development and Monitoring, 1981). Of that total of $40.6 million for estuarine research, the academic community was granted $14 million, or 37 percent of all Federal estuarine research funds. Thirty-seven percent of the funds resulted in 77 percent of the published articles.

I suspect the percentage that goes to academic institutions has declined since that time. Even if it has not, there has been a definite shift away from basic to what is euphemistically called "applied" or "goal-oriented" research. I would remind you of something Louis Pasteur pointed out: "To him who devotes his life to science, nothing can give more happiness than increasing the number of discoveries. But his cup of joy is full when the results of his studies find practical application. *There are not two sciences. There is only one science and the application of science, and these two activities are linked as the fruit is to the tree.*"

I would like to close with a statement by the famous Baltimorean, H.L. Mencken, "Every human situation has a simple solution — neat, plausible and wrong." He was right — at least as far as estuaries are concerned.

REFERENCES

Hoffman, T.S., D. Keyes and J.G. Titus. 1983. Projecting
Future Sea Level Rise: Methodology, Estimates to the Year
2100, and Research Needs. Environmental Protection Agency, Washington, D.C.

Interagency Committee on Ocean Pollution Research, De-
velopment, and Monitoring/Federal Council for Science,
Engineering, and Technology. 1979. Federal Plan for Ocean
Pollution Research, Development, and Monitoring, Fiscal
Years 1979-1983, 160 pp.

Interagency Committee on Ocean Pollution Research, De-
velopment, and Monitoring/Federal Council for Science,
Engineering, and Technology. 1979. Federal Plan for Ocean
Pollution Resarch, Development, and Monitoring, Fiscal
Years 1979-1983, Working Paper 1, 230 pp.

Interagency Committee on Ocean Pollution Research, Development, and Monitoring/Federal Council for Science,
Engineering, and Technology. 1979. Reports of the Sub-
committees on: National Needs and Problems; Data Collec-
tion; Storage and Distribution; Monitoring; Research and
Development, Working Papers 0-5, 177 pp.

National Academy of Sciences. 1983. Changing Climate. Report
of the Carbon Dioxide Assessment Committee, National
Academy of Sciences, Washington, D.C.

Officer, C.B., L.E. Cronin, R.B. Biggs and J.H. Ryther. 1981. A perspective on estuarine and coastal research funding. Environmental Science and Technology 15:1282-1285.

Pritchard, D.W. 1967. What is an estuary: physical viewpoint. Pages 3-5 in: G.H. Lauff (ed.), Estuaries, American Association for the Advancement of Science, Washington, D.C.

Schneider, S.H. and R. Londer. 1984. The Coevolution of Climate and Life. Sierra Club Books, San Francisco, CA.

Schubel, J.R. 1981. The Living Chesapeake. The Johns Hopkins University Press, Baltimore, MD.